Syllable Zen

Corrina Thompson

BookLeaf Publishing

India | USA | UK

Presentation by *BookLeaf Publishing*

Web: www.bookleafpub.com

E-mail: info@bookleafpub.com

ISBN: 9789360940829

First edition 2024

PREFACE

In the quiet spaces between moments, where words fade and silence speaks, the contemplative haiku poet finds solace. Each syllable a universe, each verse a window into the soul's landscape. In this collection of haiku, I invite you to join me in the gentle dance of reflection, where simplicity reveals the profound, and each poem is a stepping stone on the path to inner peace.
-Corrina

Downstream

The constant current
Always moving, takes my pain
Forever downstream

Adventure

2

Adventure awaits
Not knowing what I would find
I ended up here

Reflection

3

A drop of water
In it is her reflection
Vaporized by night

Reach

Where the sky meets trees
Is a place that begs for me
To wander, to reach

Mosaic

I may be broken
But today I choose to love
My mosaic heart

I am

6

In my mind's third eye
I feel. I believe. I am.
What I cannot see

Wind

The wind brings wisdom
From every yesterday
As it whips through time

Heaven

8

Just where is heaven?
Is it in the wispy clouds?
Or here, in my heart?

See

9

Dropped before my eyes
Something I couldn't un-feel
And now, I can see

Unafraid

A blade of grass, green
Paralyzed by winter's frost
Awakes, unafraid

Dust

Unfurl to the world
Perfect and pure, soon to be
Ethereal dust

Activation

12

Moonlit vibration
Cosmic illumination
Soul activation

Spring

13

The tender shoreline
Punctuated with cool air
And notions of Spring

Shine

This, beyond the clouds
A bright, magnetic life force
Lives to shine again

Still

15

On this sweet morning
The butterflies flutter by
And my heart is still

Roses

She smells the roses
In her magical pink robe
To her heart's content

You

The trajectory
A long, meandering path
Always leads to You

Stars

18

Sunset settles in
The wonderments of today
Twinkle with the stars

Sycamore

19

The old sycamore
Larger than life in his death
Finds purpose at rest

Canvas

The whimsical clouds
Are a moving exhibit
On the sky's canvas

Born

Poetically
The syllables are racing
A haiku is born